Red Lotus
Buddhist Wisdom

By Domo Geshe Rinpo

D1248806

Other books by Domo Geshe Rinpoche
Mystery of Emptiness & Love
ISBN 978-0-692-00394-7

Hermitage Buddhist Publishing
PO Box 126
Neillsville, WI 54456
hermitagebuddhistpublishing@gmail.com

www.white-conch.org

Library of Congress registered copyright 2009
Tara Wangchuk,
Domo Geshe Rinpoche
ISBN: 978-0-692-00410-4

> *Dedicated to every meditator*
> *who has opened their wisdom eye*
> *and sees the real lotus*

Thank you to Ani Ngawang Khandro (Julie Allon) for your untiring
efforts in bringing this book to blossom.
Thank you also to Ani Ngawang Gema (Sarah Buchler) for your editing skill
and to many others who helped gather and select quotations.
Thank you, the wonderful photographers of Dreamstime Photos
Back cover photo credit Eclectic Visions, Rachel Balunsat

Lotus and symbols

"As a lotus flower is born in water, grows in water and rises out of water to stand above it unsoiled, so I, born in the world, raised in the world, having overcome the world, live unsoiled by the world."

The Buddha

The lotus, as king of flowers, is a symbol of purity and peace. It is also a sign of the victory of purity in rising above the elements from which it came. Its effortless emergence from the muck demonstrates how we can transcend our own discontented circumstances.

The lotus is one of the most beloved symbols in the Orient, where they grow abundantly in humid places. Not only are lotuses dramatic and beautiful, they also inspire and uplift us spiritually.

Moreover, the lotus is a powerful visual symbol that displays transcendence of worldly attachment. It arises in a new form that is delightfully different than its source elements; seed, mud and sunlight. Even when the petals are gone, a rare beauty remains.

The seedpod of the lotus flower produces especially attractive and hard seeds prized by Buddhists and used as prayer beads. While reciting the mantra of the Buddha of Compassion, Avalokitesvara (Tib Chenrizig), the secret of new growth contained within is nurtured as the seed of enlightenment within the meditator's lotus heart. The mantra, "Om Mani Pedme Hum" stimulates our compassion and carries the message of loving kindness and freedom to all living beings in the myriad realms. The literal translation of the mantra from the Sanskrit is "Hail to the Jewel in the Lotus."

The number of lotus petals also corresponds to the visualized lotus chakras or centers within the practitioner. The thirty-two petals at the root center, sixty-four at the navel, eight at the heart, sixteen at the throat, thirty-two at the crown and two at the brow relate to the psychophysical nervous system in certain meditation practices.

The lotus is also the inspiration for the fluid and elegant sacred mudra, the Tibetan Buddhist hand gesture of creating the lotus. The lotus mudra corresponds to high spiritual states of mind.

In Buddhist iconography, deities are seated on precious cushions of fully blossoming lotuses. Lotus thrones are the most perfect seats we can offer and also describe the deity as a fully enlightened being. In ancient times, so few people could read that the visual representations of deities educated them about the qualities possessed by particular deities. Individual Buddhas and Bodhisattvas were identified with unique mudras, implements, colors, posture and more. For example, Chenrizig, the Buddha of Compassion, holds a lotus, showing that he belongs to the Padma (lotus) family associated with Buddha

Amitabha, one of the five dyani, or meditation Buddha families.

The red lotus symbolizes love, compassion and passion. In its rare form, it is called red utpala lotus. Kurukulla, a female dakini, holds her special implements, a bow and arrow, fashioned completely from red lotuses. Red Tara has a red utpala lotus blooming at her left shoulder to show her rare and valuable quality and her place in the Padma family.

A white lotus represents spiritual perfection and total purity. It is often associated with White Tara, one of the three long life Buddhas, of whom the others are Amatayus and Nangyalma.

The pink lotus displays enlightenment and is often used as a seat or is seen blossoming at shoulder height of a deity, sometimes mixed with rainbow hues.

A blue lotus, a rare form called utpala, is said to bloom

only once in a hundred years. This variety is a signature symbol of Chittamani Tara, the highest yoga tantra form of beloved Green Tara, the female Buddha said to be Mother of all the Buddhas.

Most Buddhas and deities sit in a special posture called the full lotus, each foot resting on the thigh of the other leg. Meditators emulate this posture of dignified and disciplined purity of character to allow the natural energy of the body to align with inner energies for advanced practice. For those of us who cannot see the deities so clearly or assume a full lotus posture for hours and hours, there are other meditations more compatible with our nature.

Even though it might seem that enlightenment is far away, we cannot judge our own progress. If we sit by the side of a lotus pond to observe a lotus emerging, the bud forming and growing tall, its petals opening to full development, it will seem as though nothing is happening. The movements of growth are imperceptible to our senses. Like that, our spiritual growth can be imperceptible to us, but day by day, we approach our own full flowering.

Tendrel – the unspoken

The delicate beautiful lotus further inspires us to search for our own truth, to discover what is real in a mass of contradictory appearances. We might turn to books and the world of ideas for fresh inspiration. We will discover, as did the ancient philosophers, that the nature of reality is emptiness, absolutely devoid of illusion and appearance. Without serving as a support for phenomena or manifestation, emptiness is simply how all things exist in their deep nature.

However, Buddhism further describes what we perceive as the world around us, our bodies, and even our minds as dependent origination. All things come into being by depending on other things, that is, causes and conditions. Only in this manner can they exist at all. A theoretically permanent and independent thing could not interact with anything else without becoming changed itself. An object cannot touch anything without losing the supposed qualities of permanence and independent existence, and is therefore a fantasy.

Tendrel is a Tibetan word indicating the interconnectedness of phenomena, but tendrel is even more than that. Tendrel is a powerful, inclusive concept that acts upon all of us in a nonverbal manner, connecting us to the unseen energy of the world and those around us in a marvelous, organic, symbiotic dance of manifestation. To connect with the tendrel means that not only do we arise in harmony with the world around us simply by our presence, but our motivation and actions affect the tendrel dynamic in ways unseen, but not unfelt. To be effective in life, rather than seeking a forced peace with the world, we should seek to affect the tendrel of our existence in ways that cause change harmoniously.

Symbols, such as the lotus, used to connect with tendrel are valid tools that help us access wisdom-based inter-connectedness with the invisible world beyond the abilities of ordinary mind. Even without conscious efforts, the non-verbal link between a visual object and a reality that exists in a hidden form bypasses the way we usually process data. This is why symbols affect us so strongly.

About the quotations

Over a number of years, my students have shared my quotations with each other and have requested many times to see them in book form. I have enjoyed presenting them here in a more contemporary manner with my original graphics. In my book *Mystery of Emptiness & Love,* many concepts that are presented here in short, easy to remember forms are expanded.

Key subjects of the innate view, subtle mind, emptiness, and compassion are discussed at length. Please read this more comprehensive text to increase your understanding of these important concepts. I also recommend that you read books written by His Holiness the Dalai Lama to learn more about Buddhism.

Now we turn our attention to the specific form of wisdom in short passages or aphorisms. The Buddha said, "*In the sky, there is no distinction of east and west. People create distinctions out of their own minds and then believe them to be true.*" This means that there is absolutely nothing to cling to as permanent even if we believe it is real. Even open, unimpeded space is not permanent because the fallacy of directionality is based upon illusory principles constructed for convenience and lacks a basis in reality. However, over time, deep reliance will accumulate toward conventional concepts, imbuing them with a perceptual-based solidity that they do not possess. We are touching upon it briefly but there is so much more to discover in this aphorism.

Another important saying of the Buddha is, "*As the fletcher whittles and makes straight his arrows, so the master directs his straying thoughts.*" This quotation is important enough to have endured more than 2,500 years, translated into hundreds of languages.

These insights, connected to a path of transformation, are distilled concepts properly used as memory devices for meditation. We consider wisdom sayings very differently than quips we find to amuse ourselves only to forget them as soon as we turn the page.

In Buddhism, we cultivate high regard for The Buddha, The Dharma, and The Sangha, known collectively as the Three Jewels of Refuge. In fact, we hold them in such high regard that if we want to swear, we take the name of the Three Jewels in vain. This is how important they are! You have to really feel upset to say, "*Three Jewels!*"

It comes out like, *"Holy Jesus!"* So, now you know how to swear in Tibetan.

Joking aside, wisdom quotations are called gems because they are valuable, even beyond calculation. In ancient times, gems were believed to hold special magical powers. Like that, Dharma sayings are believed to hold power. Just to memorize them and to hold them in our mind, recalling them at the right moment when guidance is needed, gives us a sense of the protection provided by these marvelous insights.

Of the three jewels, Buddha, Dharma, and Sangha, Buddha means "awakened one", or the nature of the awakened mind. The Dharma is the body of teachings of the Buddha and the Path to the awakened state. The Sangha is the community of beings who follow the teachings, rely on the awakening mind, and in turn, become enlightened themselves.

It might seem that the Sangha is not as important, but if the Buddha and the Dharma existed without the Sangha, it would be like attending a school where no one ever graduated! Sangha is our hope for the future, needed to help others become free. The very nature and essence of the Sangha means that somebody did it, and so can we!

The Dharma jewel is beyond value and is always changing as it comes into creative contact with suffering living beings. Since we do not know what kinds of activities living beings will need in the future, the Dharma jewel must be infinitely flexible and responsive, active in highly skillful methods that are alive in the modern world.

We do not know what problems might be encountered 500 years from now. Maybe the earth will be covered by water with only 50 square miles of land, as some scientists today tell us. Perhaps the polar ice caps will be gone and people will live on boats. If so, you may need to learn to be a good sailor. In this case, most of our worldly wisdom will be about wind, waves, and weather. In the future, perhaps you and I will stand together on a sailing ship discussing Buddhism by relating the inner winds of the human body and the winds that blow across the vast ocean of our new world.

How to use these Buddhist quotations

There are three methods we can use to gain the most value from quotations or short aphorisms. First, we can memorize distilled wisdom sayings and fix them within our mind in a prepared dharmic environment. Using sayings as tools to understand other concepts is actually the traditional method in monastic training.

Aphorisms and sayings of The Buddha become even more important in the formal logic used in Tibetan monastery education. We must be able to defend our own positions in a formal manner by giving scriptural references in the correct context to convince others that our knowledge is coherent.

However, even someone without the benefits of a monastery education can memorize short passages of scripture. Hold them in a sacred place in your own mind where you maintain high motivation. Respect yourself as well as the real you deep inside.

Another method of utilizing wisdom from these sayings is to meditate on the aphorisms. We must first make a distinction between worldly gems of wisdom and Dharma gems of wisdom that lead to liberation, giving special respect to the latter. The purpose of meditating on wisdom sayings is to give structure and coherence to our personal process. Sometimes, we may be uncertain about the meaning of a Buddhist concept. We might make guesses as we tend toward thinking ideas are either true or not true before we have made a final determination. Only through meditation and contemplation will we have a chance to understand the author's intention. For example, *"Peace comes from within. Do not seek it without."* The author is Lord Buddha Shakyamuni. However, what was the author's intention?

We can go inside our sacred heart meditation space with awareness and have an imaginary conversation with The Buddha. We engage in a soft and alive inquiry, *"What could you possibly mean, Lord Buddha?"* Another way to discover The Buddha's intention is to think, *'What was the Buddha's agenda?'* The Buddha did have an agenda. What do you think? *"Peace comes from within. Do not seek it without."* What was his motivation?

Shantideva, a Buddhist sage who wrote, *"Guide to the Bodhisattva's Way of Life"* 1200 years ago, also had a special agenda. He wanted to help others achieve development of compassion and did this by describing in detail how bodhisattvas behave. However, even those who are not yet bodhisattvas or enlightened beings can take Shantideva's advice seriously, modeling their behavior and thinking after Shantideva's high ideals. This is the human process of becoming an enlightened, beneficial bodhisattva hero.

When meditating on an aphorism, it is helpful to understand exactly what error it addresses and corrects. When this is accomplished, the clarity and sparkle of a Dharma jewel becomes a healing remedy against a particular fault. For example, *"In the sky, there is no distinction of east and west. People create distinctions out of their own minds and then believe them to be true."* What is the error addressed here?

"As the fletcher whittles and makes straight his arrows, so the master directs his straying thoughts." This is actually a quote from Buddha Shakyamuni, but let us suppose for a moment Nagarjuna made this statement. If Nagarjuna, the great Middle Way philosopher on emptiness, said this, what would his agenda have been,

what would he want us to think?

What is the error that is remedied here? How would the meditation inspired by Nagarjuna be different from the meditation inspired by The Buddha? How would Nagarjuna persuade us differently? If he had said this, I imagine that Nagarjuna would be encouraging us to swiftly cut away and remove the useless, the trivial, and the superficial. By paring down what we do not need, we eventually uncover peace of mind with fewer thoughts and higher quality thoughts.

Aphorisms continue to be rich sources of meditation material, even for advanced meditators. With courage and concentration, we can gradually direct and control our thinking so that enlightenment becomes a real possibility. The fletcher makes arrows so that they will fly straight and hit the target. New Buddhists, however, do not need to be so concerned. They could shoot quite randomly and still be successful, as errors are quite plentiful at this point.

The third way aphorisms are used effectively is as remembrances of the sequence of our formal practice. Written meditation practices and prayers are guided remembrances of the order of practice, useful when we cannot mentally retain the concepts that align us with higher development. Dharma gems of wisdom, the lines of our blessed daily recitations and prayers that we memorize and hold in spiritual perspective, are wisdom already alive in us. I have many students who say that they wake up joyfully in the middle of the night reciting lines of their meditation practice.

It is true that something comes alive in us when we remember the structure of a higher functioning model, for example, Geshe Chekawa's *"Seven Point Mind Training:"*

"Ponder that all phenomena are like a dream.

Discern the basic nature of awareness that has no arising.

The opponent itself liberates itself in its own place.

Between sessions, act like an illusory person.

In regard to the three objects, three roots of what is constructive."

These lines are refined devices meant to be held separately and in sequence. They are developmental steps toward arising compassion in order to do tonglen, a Tibetan giving and taking technique. This breath and heart-based practice is used for the healing of ourselves and others.

In conclusion, to gain the most benefit from prayer, recitation practice and reading scriptures, we need to develop a fresh and new admiration for the worded nature of our practices.

Of course, we already profoundly respect the wordless basis and nature of enlightened mind. We might even wish to emulate this state by not thinking anything at all, abiding in wordless peace by just sitting without allowing the mind to move at all. However, this actually does not work.

Instead, our busy minds need nutritious content on the way to transformation. We are like caterpillars transmuting to a completely new way of being. We need many kinds of encouragement to nourish our deeper inner minds, where we are more alive in what some might even call a soul.

I hope that these contemporary Buddhist quotations compiled in Red Lotus will stimulate your thinking so that you reflect on deeper dynamics. In this way, you will begin to establish the important stable basis needed so that enlightenment can blossom like a pure lotus. Whether Buddhist or not, please enjoy what is offered here in the spirit of joy, friendship and love.

May the dharma come alive in you
and may abundant happiness

follow   you   like   the   finest   perfume

My highest motivation should be bodhichitta

the strong and vibrant

living wish to see

and facilitate

the end of suffering

of every single sentient being,

whether I have met them or not

Change is not the enemy

Change is how you are alive

May I be like
the bright full moon,
my face reflecting the sun
of the Buddha's teachings
to those standing
in front of me

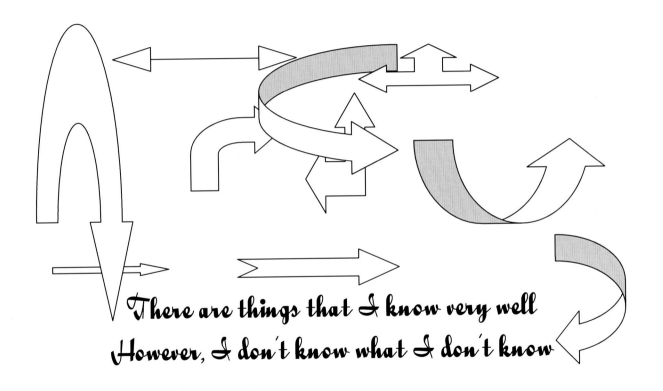

There are things that I know very well
However, I don't know what I don't know

After training the mind... in calm and introspective thinking...admire that quality in yourself   Aft

training   ining t

mind... i

After training the mind in calm and introspective thinking...admire that quality in yourself   und...

ntrospective thinking...admire that quality in yourself   After training the mind... in calm and introspecti

admire that quality in yourself   After training the mind... in calm . . . and introspective thinking...adm

that quality in .... yourself   After training the mind... in calm and introspective thinking...admire th

quality in yourself   After training the mind in calm and introspective thinking . . . admire that quality

After training the mind... in calm and introspective thinking...admire that quality in yourself   Af

training the mind... in calm and introspective thinking...admire that quality in yourself   After training t

mind... in calm and introspective thinking...admire that quality in yourself   After training the mind...

After training the mind... in calm and introspective thinking...admire that quality in yourself   Af

Now make effort to return to the effortless state

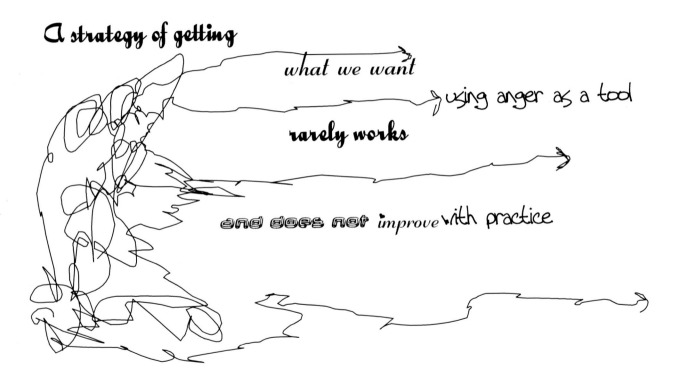

A strategy of getting what we want using anger as a tool rarely works and does not improve with practice

The Tin Rule is me first

The Silver Rule is you first

The Golden Rule is all of us first

Yes...

life is

illusory

but the lessons are real

Excitement
and a bright
fresh feeling comes

when I make deliberate choices
to see the Path of transformation
as dear and loving toward me

Reincarnation?

It doesn't matter if you believe in it or not
Someday you will find out for sure!

The powerful self-respect
developed in dharma practice
gives us an opportunity
to work with ego
in a way
that will completely change
the way that we perceive our world
～～～～～～～～～～～～～～～～

For the better!!

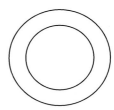

 Effort without patience is blame
Effort with patience is a mind that delights in virtue

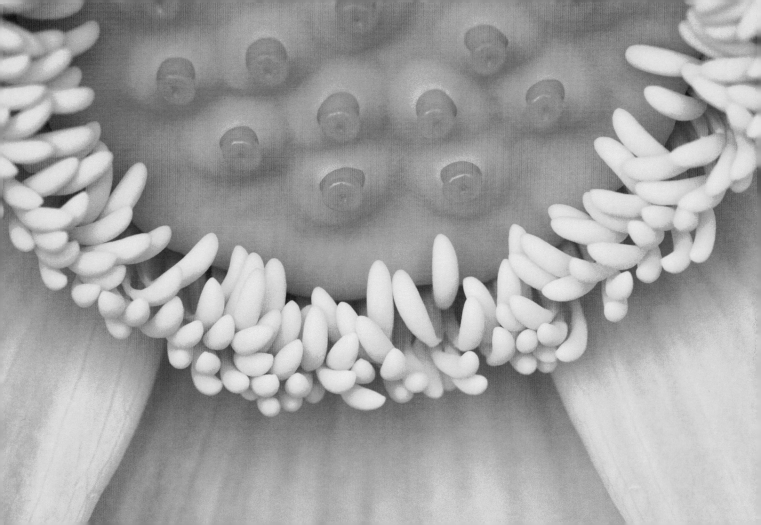

We can also experience

Buddha's love

while we are on the path to enlightenment

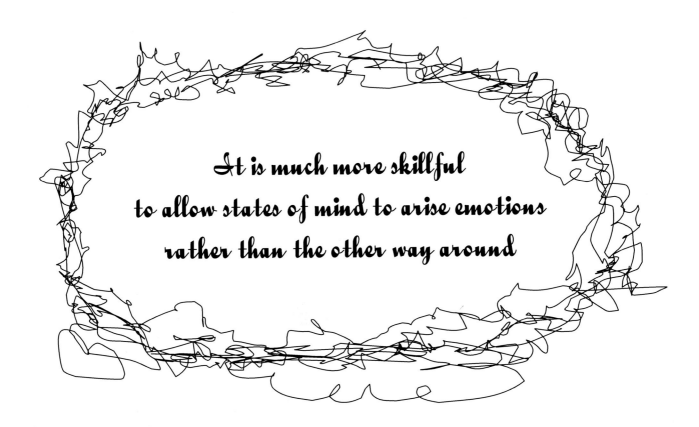

It is much more skillful
to allow states of mind to arise emotions
rather than the other way around

I am my best when I am not looking at myself but at others

Meditation
heals from the
inside out

Real music is like the Great Path of Dharma

The art of a great teacher is to solidify it just enough
and invite those who cannot hear the inner music to step onto the ice

Then the ice disappears and they are carried away by the true river!

Kindness is applied compassion

If we are disappointed by someone
and spread disappointment
toward others in general,
why not see them
as a point of reference
for our compassion practice?

To push them away in aversion
might cause us to lose a treasure of patience

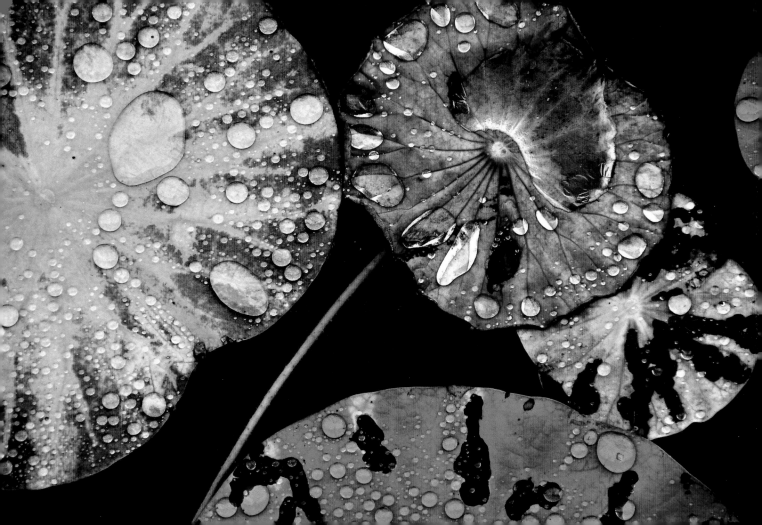

The ceaseless movements of compassion....

are like storms on the sun...

throwing off enormous energies

in response

to the needs

of living beings

Past and future are only tools we use to interact with the world
but only the flow of moments of NOW make it possible to be alive

So, we have two forms of present moment;
An ability to manipulate perceptions such as past present and future,
or interacting with the energy of the world with our inner life process

Both are important, but for higher development, the second is supreme

On the path

to enlightenment,

move carefully

through this world

like a guest

Create as much

benefit as possible

while you are here!

First gain **serious preparation** for transcendence
step by step

After entering the awakened enlightened state,
you will **laugh and laugh**

The illusory suffering state
never was,
is not now,
and never will be real!

There is a dynamic tension

between who you are right now

and the possibilities of

who

you

could

be

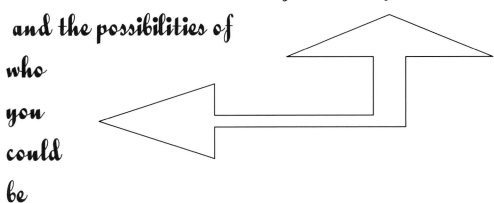

Can you feel it?

We think magical events are unusual

However, *magical events*
happen in our minds continuously
because we perceive the world like a fantasy

Subtle is stronger

It may seem like subtle minds
           are of little importance
                       as hardly there at all

but ordinary, denser mind is
                       weak by comparison

Habitually, we use ordinary mind
instead of relying on subtle objects such as Buddhas and Bodhisattvas

Great guidance beings are more alive in subtle places,
this is where actual practices are alive

There is no difference between
you and the awakened Buddha
except for your perceptions

I wish all my dear mothers of all my previous lives
easy journey to the vast
awakened state

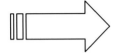 Holding away change

and demanding
life to be like it was before,

rubs and irritates the actual way you are alive
like petting a cat from tail to head

The Buddha did not come
to help you feel better.
He came to set you free

Every living being <u>must</u> become free

The compassion of the Buddhas and Bodhisattvas will <u>not</u> be thwarted!

May I become a golden fountain,

a hidden well
and a silvery spring,
each flowing wisdom's nectar
in accordance with the needs of living beings

The teachings
of Lord Buddha Shakyamuni
come alive with a correct love dynamic
with the Path to enlightenment

You are a human being

with a mind, body, and karma of a human being

This is your present circumstance

Therefore, this is your diamond realm and you are lucky

You are not presently a god

so the value of the god realm is nothing

by comparison to what you have in the palm of your hand

Peace is the result of balanced energies

The healing preparation for transformation is hard work,
not in itself a peaceful process

So, when times of peace come, we enjoy

then continue working
on the obstacles that lie beneath the veneer of peace...

and on and on it goes!

Meditation is my

special time

to nurture a promise to myself
to become new in a way
that cannot be done with
exercise, good nutrition
or even loving relationships

The ego, a kind of organizational principle,
needs to be healthy, flexible,
and
strong enough
to withstand and flow with
the rigors of preparation
for transformation

The beaten down ego is useless!

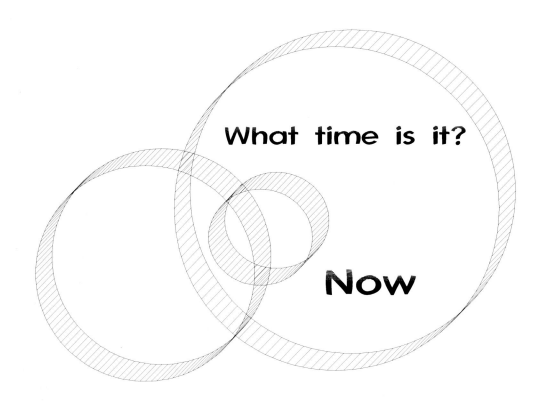

What time is it?

Now

Like a song singing beginning to end,
and end to beginning simultaneously,
the Path to perfection exists simultaneously,
but in time and space becomes linear

A conductor
rehearses the dissonant elements
of a discordant symphony,
holding them together
by swinging a baton to gain their attention

Like this, the self uses the ego
to stabilize and accomplish life's tasks

When
I sit
for meditation,
I am standing
For what I believe in

Anticipate the call of higher being calling us to awakening

Practice by standing at the inner door

Like someone waiting for a knock of a beloved friend

Teachings of Buddhism

help break down the misunderstanding

between how I actually exist,

how I **think** I exist,

and how I exist in my *fantasies*

From the vast enlightened
sphere of beneficial intention...

a bodhisattva hero is born

Wisdom without compassion is dry

compassion without wisdom is foolishness

The Fifth Turning
of the Wheel of Dharma
will only happen in your heart!

Your self-induced glass ceiling is limiting your progress
However, if you practice meditation enthusiastically,
your fingerprints are all over it

Many good people do not begin meditation until middle age,
but suffer because they did not start sooner.

Make sincere apology to the heart being,
not you but the real you.

Some who do this experience a shock of joy and forgiveness!